Dad, I Want to Know You Better

A Father's Guided Keepsake Journal to
Share His Memories and Life

Producer & International Distributor
eBookPro Publishing
www.ebook-pro.com

Dad, I Want to Know You Better
Made Easy Press

Copyright © 2022 Made Easy Press

All rights reserved; No parts of this book may be reproduced or transmitted in any form or by any means, electronic or mechanical, including photocopying, recording, taping, or by any information retrieval system, without the author's explicit permission in writing.

Written by Dani Silas
Design by Natalie Lukatsky

Contact: agency@ebook-pro.com

Contents

A Letter to My Dad 9

About Me 13

Our Family Tree 14

The Year I Was Born 16

Family 20

Early Life and Childhood 28

Growing Up 38

Work 44

Love and Marriage 50

Fatherhood 66

Who I Am Now 74

My Favorites 76

Would You Rather 80

Top 5 82

Looking Back 90

My Wishes for You 96

A Letter to My Dear Child 99

> "*My father gave me the greatest gift anyone could give another person, he believed in me.*"
>
> – Jim Valvano

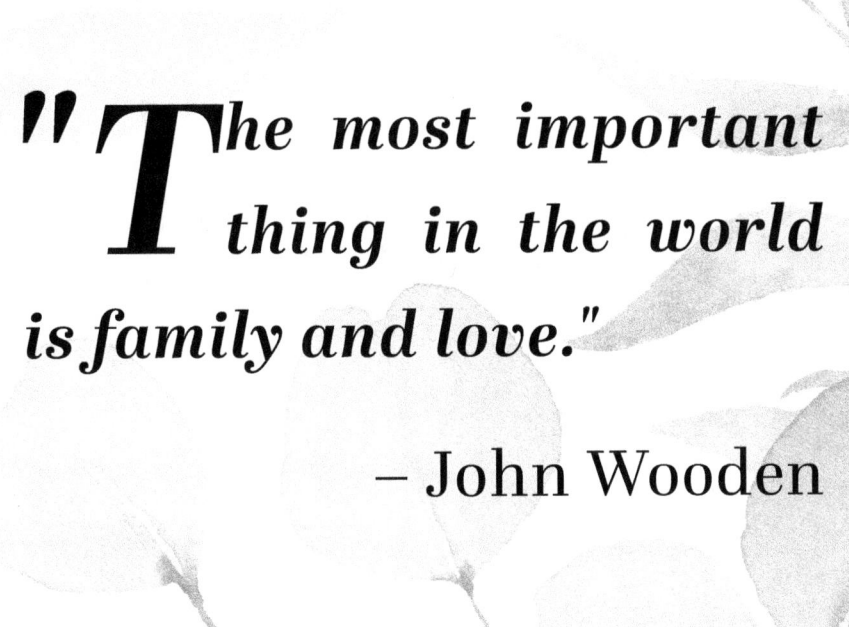

"The most important thing in the world is family and love."

– John Wooden

This Book Belongs To...

....

A Letter to My Dad

Sign your name

"Being a great father is like shaving. No matter how good you shaved today, you have to do it again tomorrow."

— Reed Markham

"Fathers, like mothers, are not born."

– David Gottesman

About Me

Full Name

Date of Birth

Zodiac Sign

Height

Hair Color

Eye Color

Distinguishing Marks

Languages I speak

Our Family Tree

_____ _____
My Great-   **My Great-**
Grandfather   **Grandfather**

_____ _____
My Great-   **My Great-**
Grandmother   **Grandmother**

_____ _____
My Grandmother   My Grandfather

_____
My Mother

_____ _____ _____
Me   My Sibling   My Sibling

_____   _____
**My Great-   My Great-
Grandfather**   Grandfather**

_____   _____
**My Great-   My Great-
Grandmother**   Grandmother**

_____   _____
My Grandmother   My Grandfather

_____
My Father

_____   _____   _____
My Sibling   My Sibling   My Sibling

The Year I Was Born...

Who was the leader of your country?
_____

Who was the mayor of your city?
_____

Which celebrities were born in the same year?
_____
_____
_____
_____

Were there any big scientific discoveries?
_____
_____
_____
_____

Were there any important inventions?
_____
_____
_____
_____

Were there any important events happening in the world?

___

Which memorable movies came out?

___

Did anyone famous pass away?

___

What was the price of a carton of milk?

___

Picture Gallery

Childhood Photo

Place your childhood photo here

Family Photo

Place your family photo here

Family

What are your parents' names?

_____

How old were they when you were born?

_____

What were their professions?

_____
_____

Who do you take after most in looks?

_____
_____

Which physical attributes do you share?

_____
_____

Who do you take after most in personality?

_____
_____

Which qualities or attributes do you share?

_____
_____

What are your grandparents' names?

_____

_____

Did you know them?

_____

_____

Did your grandparents live close by? How often did you see them?

_____

_____

Do you have any treasured memories with your grandparents?

_____

_____

_____

_____

How many siblings do you have?

_____

What are their names?

_____

Where are you in order of birth?

_____

Which sibling looks most similar to you?

_____

Which sibling is most like you in personality?

_____

How was your relationship with your siblings growing up?

_____

_____

Has your relationship with your siblings changed throughout your life? If so, in what way?

_____

_____

What is your favorite childhood memory with your siblings?

_____

_____

What did you like to do together when you were younger?

_____

Do you have any brothers-or-sisters-in-law? What are their names?

_____

_____

How did they and your siblings meet?

_____

_____

Do you have any nieces and nephews? What are their names?

_____

_____

How old were you when your first niece or nephew was born?

_____

Did you ever babysit or look after them?

_____

_____

Did you see them often when they were children?

_____

What special memories do you have with your nieces and nephews?

_____

_____

_____

Do you have any aunts and uncles? What are their names?

_____

_____

How is your relationship with your aunts and uncles?

_____
_____
_____

Do you have any cousins? What are their names?

_____
_____

Did you grow up close by to any of your cousins?

_____
_____
_____

Are there any cousins you have a particularly close relationship with?

_____
_____
_____

What are some favorite memories with your extended family?

_____
_____
_____
_____
_____

Share a Family Recipe

_____

Ingredients:

_____
_____
_____
_____

Instructions:

_____
_____
_____
_____
_____
_____
_____
_____
_____
_____

> "*Fathering is not something perfect men do, but something that perfects the man.*"

– Frank Pittman

"*It is a wise father that knows his own child.*"

– William Shakespeare

Early Life and Childhood
Birth

Where were you born?
_____

How close to your due date were you born?
_____

How much did you weigh at birth?
_____

What was your length?
_____

What was the full name you were given?
_____
_____

Were you named after anyone? If so, whom?
_____
_____

Did you have a nickname as a baby?
_____

Have you always liked your name?

_____

_____

Were you the firstborn or did you have siblings?

_____

How did your family celebrate your birth?

_____

_____

_____

What stories does your family tell about your birth?

_____

_____

_____

_____

How did your parents describe you as a baby?

_____

_____

_____

_____

Firsts

When did you first grab a toy?
_____

When did you first smile?
_____

When did you first laugh?
_____

When did you first roll over?
_____

When did you first sit up unsupported?
_____

When did you first crawl?
_____

When did you first stand?
_____

When did you first walk?
_____

When did you say your first word?
_____

What was your first word?

_____

What was the first solid food you ate?

_____

Childhood

What is your earliest memory?

_____

_____

_____

Did you have a nickname as a child?

_____

At what age did you first go to kindergarten? Do you remember anything about it?

_____

_____

_____

Who were your best friends as a small child?

_____

Where did you go to elementary school?

_____

Who were your first school friends?

_____

_____

What was the name of your first-grade teacher? Did you like him/her?

_____

What was your favorite subject in elementary school?

_____

What was your least favorite subject?

_____

What did you excel at?

_____

What did you like to do during recess?

_____

Did you play any sports or instruments?

_____

_____

Which other hobbies did you have as a child?

_____

_____

What did your childhood room look like? Did you share with anyone?

_____

_____

_____

What is your favorite memory from elementary school?

_____

_____

_____

_____

Who was your favorite teacher at school?

_____

_____

How did you celebrate your early birthdays?

_____

_____

_____

_____

What is your favorite birthday memory?

_____

_____

_____

_____

What is your favorite childhood holiday memory?

_____

_____

_____

_____

Where did your family go on vacations?

_____

_____

_____

_____

Did your family have any pets? What were their names? Who was in charge of them?

_____

_____

_____

What were you afraid of as a child?

_____
_____
_____
_____

What did you most love to do?

_____
_____
_____
_____

What did you most love to eat?

_____
_____
_____

Which family members were you particularly close with?

_____
_____
_____
_____

"I love my mother and father. The older I get, the more I value everything that they gave me."

– Liev Schreiber

*"**D**ads are most ordinary men turned by love into heroes, adventurers, story-tellers, and singers of song."*

– Pam Brown

Growing Up

Where did you go to middle school?
_____

Where did you go to high school?
_____

What was your favorite subject in high school?
_____

What was your least favorite subject?
_____

Who was your favorite teacher? What do you remember about him/her?
_____
_____
_____

Which extracurricular activities did you participate in?
_____
_____
_____

Did your school have a mascot or school colors? What were they?
_____
_____
_____

Did you have a school uniform? What did it look like?

_____

_____

Did you play any sports or instruments in high school?

_____

_____

_____

What did you like to do outside of school?

_____

_____

_____

Who were your best friends as a teenager?

_____

_____

What did you like to do with your friends?

_____

_____

_____

Did you go on dates in high school?

_____

_____

_____

Did you have a curfew?

___

Did your parents give you an allowance? If so, how much was it?

___

Did you have any chores around the house? Which ones?

___

___

Did you enjoy your chores?

___

When did you get your driver's license?

___

How many times did you take the driver's test before you passed?

___

Who helped you learn to drive?

___

Did you like driving?

___

Did you have your own car as a teenager?

___

What was your relationship with your family like as a teenager?

___

___

___

What kind of clothes were in style when you were a teen?

_____

_____

Is there a fashion style from your childhood that you particularly miss?

_____

_____

What kind of music was popular then?

_____

_____

Was there anything you didn't appreciate as a teen but can see the value of today?

_____

_____

_____

What did you like to do on weekends?

_____

_____

Who was your favorite musician?

_____

_____

Did you ever see any musicians live in concert?

_____

Did you ever attend a music festival?

_____

How did you celebrate your birthday in your teen years?

_____

_____

Did you have a sweet sixteen / quinceanera / bar/bat mitzvah, or some other special celebration? How did you celebrate it?

_____

_____

_____

_____

Which subjects did you take in high school?

_____

_____

_____

How did you do on your final exams?

_____

_____

Did you acquire a high school diploma?

_____

_____

_____

_____

Did you have a graduation ceremony?
_____

How was it?
_____
_____
_____

Did you attend prom?
_____

Where was it?
_____

Did you enjoy it?
_____
_____
_____

Who did you go with?
_____
_____

What did you wear?
_____
_____
_____

Work

What was your very first job?

_____

_____

How much did it pay?

_____

How did you get it?

_____

_____

Did you enjoy the work?

_____

What do you feel like you learned from that first job?

_____

_____

_____

Which jobs did you have as a teenager?

_____

_____

_____

_____

Did you ever have an unpaid temp job? What was it?

_____

_____

What was your dream job growing up?

_____

What was the first job you held where you felt truly independent?

_____

What was the shortest job you ever held?

_____

What was the longest job you ever held?

_____

What was your favorite job?

_____

What were your work hours most of your life?

_____

Did you work as a salaried employee or were you self-employed?

_____

Who was your favorite boss?

_____

_____

Who was your least favorite boss?

_____

_____

Did you have coworkers who became good friends?

_____

_____

_____

Did you have any coworkers you didn't get along with? Why?

_____

_____

_____

When interviewing for a job, what things was it important to you to say about yourself?

_____

_____

_____

_____

Share Your Favorite Childhood Prank

_____
_____
_____
_____
_____
_____
_____
_____
_____
_____
_____
_____
_____
_____
_____
_____

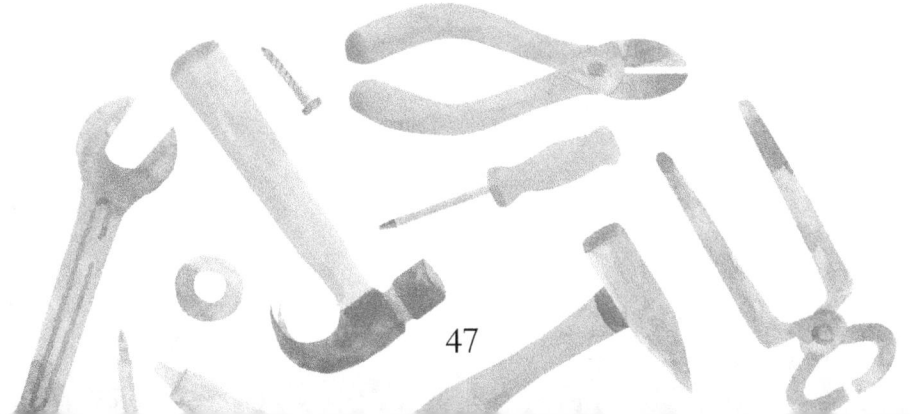

"There is no leadership more important than parenthood."

– Sheri L. Dew

"Of all the titles I've been privileged to have, 'Dad' has been always the best."

– Ken Norton

Love and Marriage
Young Love and Dating

Who was your first ever crush? Did they know or was it a secret?
_____
_____

Who did you go on your first date with?
_____

Where did you go and what did you do?
_____
_____
_____

How old were you?
_____

How did you meet?
_____

Who was your first kiss?
_____

Where did it happen?
_____
_____

With whom did you first fall in love?

_____

How did the two of you meet?

_____

_____

_____

What was your first impression of your current partner?

_____

_____

How did the two of you meet and where?

_____

_____

_____

Did you start dating right away or were you friends first?

_____

_____

What did you like to do most while you were going out?

_____

_____

_____

Do you believe in soul mates?

_____

_____

Picture Gallery

Couple Photo

Place your couple photo here

Wedding Photo

Place your wedding photo here

Wedding

Did you have a proposal? Where did it happen and how?

_____
_____
_____
_____
_____

What did the engagement ring look like?

_____
_____

How did you know you wanted to marry your partner?

_____
_____
_____
_____

How long had you been together before you got engaged?

_____
_____

How did you celebrate your engagement?

_____

_____

_____

Who did you tell first, and how?

_____

_____

_____

How long was your engagement?

_____

_____

Did you enjoy planning the wedding? Who helped with the arrangements?

_____

_____

When did you get married?

_____

Where was the ceremony held?

_____

Did you have a party? How did you celebrate your marriage?

_____

_____

_____

_____

Did you have bridesmaids or groomsmen? If so, who were they?

_____

_____

_____

What did they wear?

_____

_____

Did you have flower girls or ring bearers? If so, who were they?

_____

_____

What did they wear?

_____

_____

Who married you?

_____

_____

_____

Did you write your own vows? What did they say?

___

What did you wear to your wedding?

___

Were there any funny moments on your wedding day?

___

Did you have a cake?

___

Who gave speeches?

Did you receive any particularly memorable wedding gifts?

_____
_____
_____
_____

Do you have any keepsakes from the wedding?

_____
_____
_____
_____

Did you go on a honeymoon? If so, where too? Did you enjoy it?

_____
_____
_____
_____
_____
_____

Have you been married more than once? If so, to whom?

_____
_____
_____
_____
_____

Married Life

Did being married feel different in any way than before?

_____

_____

_____

Do you wear a wedding ring? If so, what does it look like?

_____

_____

What are your favorite attributes in your partner?

_____

_____

_____

_____

_____

What are their favorite attributes in you?

_____

_____

_____

_____

_____

_____

How do you celebrate your anniversaries?

_____
_____
_____
_____

What are some traditions you and your partner have?

_____
_____
_____
_____
_____
_____

Have you ever had troubles in your marriage? How did you solve them?

_____
_____
_____
_____
_____
_____
_____

What do you think are the foundations of a successful marriage?

_____

_____

_____

_____

_____

_____

_____

_____

_____

What is the best advice you can give to married couples?

_____

_____

_____

_____

_____

_____

_____

_____

_____

Do you have a favorite romantic memory?

_____
_____
_____
_____
_____
_____
_____
_____
_____

How do you feel your marriage was influenced by marriages of other people close to you?

_____
_____
_____
_____
_____
_____
_____

Share a Family Recipe

_____

Ingredients:

_____
_____
_____
_____

Instructions:

_____
_____
_____
_____
_____
_____
_____
_____
_____
_____

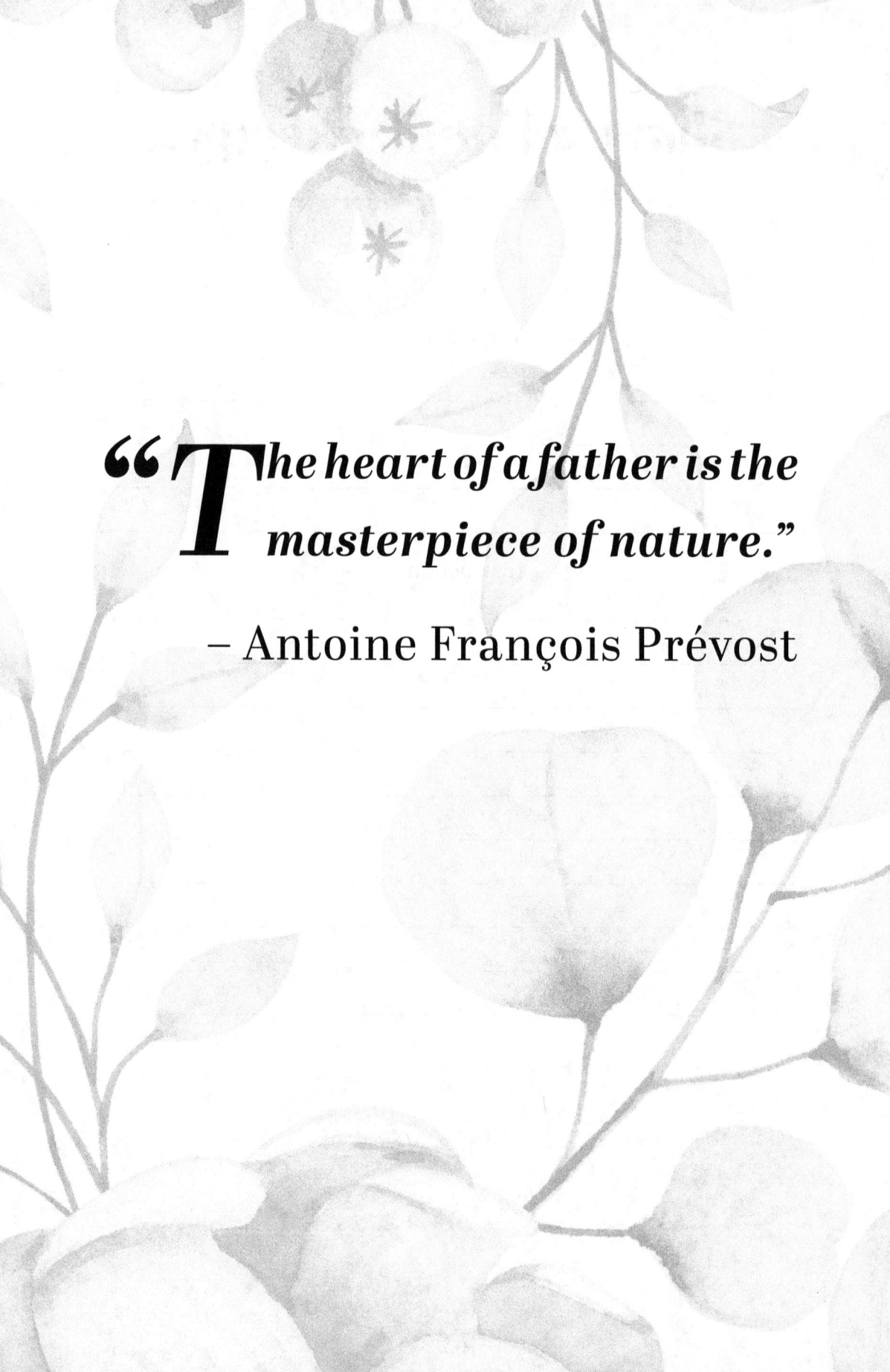

"The heart of a father is the masterpiece of nature."

– Antoine François Prévost

"The quality of a father can be seen in the goals, dreams, and aspirations he sets not only for himself but for his family"

– Reed Markham

Fatherhood

How old were you when you first became a father?

_____

How many children do you have?

_____

What are their names?

_____

_____

Were your children named after anyone? If so, whom?

_____

_____

What did it feel like to become a father?

_____

_____

Did you try for a long time before you had children?
Was it expected or unexpected?

_____

_____

_____

How were your partner's pregnancies?

_____

_____

_____

How were your birth experiences?

_____

_____

_____

_____

Did you read any books to prepare for fatherhood? If so, which?

_____

_____

_____

For each of your children, name your favorite attribute of theirs

_____

_____

_____

_____

_____

What is the best part of being a father?

_____

_____

_____

What is the most difficult part of being a father?

_____
_____
_____

Who helped you most in your early fatherhood days?

_____

Were the grandparents involved in the early days? How did they help?

_____
_____

What influences did you have in raising your children?

_____
_____
_____

Did you and your partner divide responsibilities between you when your children were young?

_____
_____
_____

Did you take time off work when your children were born?

_____
_____

Did having children impact your career? If so, how?

_____

_____

What has fatherhood taught you?

_____

_____

_____

_____

Did you have any special traditions with your children?

_____

_____

_____

Did you have a favorite book to read them or lullaby song to sing them?

_____

_____

What was your kids' bedtime routine?

_____

_____

_____

What do your children call you?

_____

What advice would you give new fathers?

_____
_____
_____
_____
_____
_____
_____
_____

What would you do differently if you could do it all again?

_____
_____
_____
_____
_____
_____
_____
_____

Share a Family Recipe

_____

Ingredients:

Instructions:

Picture Gallery

Photo with Your Children

Place a photo with your children here

Family Photo

Place your family photo here

Who I Am Now

My age

_____

Where I live

_____

My favorite way to spend the day

_____
_____
_____

My hobbies

_____
_____
_____

My best friends

_____
_____

Things that make me happy

_____
_____
_____

The places I have lived:

_____

_____

_____

The places I have traveled:

_____

_____

_____

_____

_____

My fondest memories:

_____

_____

_____

_____

_____

_____

My greatest achievements:

_____

_____

_____

_____

My Favorites

Color:
___

Meal:
___

Restaurant:
___

Cold drink:
___

Hot drink:
___

Holiday:
___

Book:
___

Movie:
___

TV show:

_____

Dessert:

_____

Sport:

_____

Actor:

_____

Board or card game:

_____

Musician:

_____

Animal:

_____

Outfit:

_____

"*Life doesn't come with an instruction book — that's why we have fathers.*"

– H. Jackson Browne

"Dad: A son's first hero, a daughter's first love."

– Unknown

Would You Rather

Cook ☐ OR Clean ☐ | Cats ☐ OR Dogs ☐

Movie ☐ OR TV show ☐ | Fancy clothes ☐ OR Pajamas ☐

Travel by plane ☐ OR Travel by boat ☐ | Endless money ☐ OR Endless time ☐

Sing ☐ OR Dance ☐ | Bath ☐ OR Shower ☐

Coffee ☐ OR Tea ☐ | Beach vacation ☐ OR Sightseeing ☐

Would You Rather

| Winter ☐ OR Summer ☐ | Sushi ☐ OR Hamburger ☐ |

| Read ☐ OR Write ☐ | Camping ☐ OR Hotel ☐ |

| Zoo ☐ OR Botanical garden ☐ | Picnic ☐ OR Restaurant ☐ |

| Hiking ☐ OR Skiing ☐ | Stay up late ☐ OR Get up early ☐ |

| Drive ☐ OR Be driven ☐ | Be able to fly ☐ OR Read minds ☐ |

Top 5

Your top 5 travel destinations:

1. _____

2. _____

3. _____

4. _____

5. _____

Your top 5 movies:

1. _____

2. _____

3. _____

4. _____

5. _____

Your top 5 books:

1. _____

2. _____

3. _____

4. _____

5. _____

Your top 5 jobs:

1. _____

2. _____

3. _____

4. _____

5. _____

Your top 5 best presents you received:

1. _____

2. _____

3. _____

4. _____

5. _____

Your top 5 meals you ever ate:

1. _____

2. _____

3. _____

4. _____

5. _____

Your top 5 vacations:

1. _____

2. _____

3. _____

4. _____

5. _____

Your top 5 most important moments:

1. _____

2. _____

3. _____

4. _____

5. _____

Your top 5 biggest successes:

1. _____

2. _____

3. _____

4. _____

5. _____

Your top 5 favorite attributes in people:

1. _____

2. _____

3. _____

4. _____

5. _____

Your top 5 funny memories:

1. _____

2. _____

3. _____

4. _____

5. _____

Your top 5 best tips for life:

1. _____

2. _____

3. _____

4. _____

5. _____

"One father is more than a hundred schoolmasters."

– George Herbert

"A father's smile has been known to light up a child's entire day."

– Susan Gale

Looking Back

What is your favorite inspirational quote?

_____
_____
_____

What do you think everyone should experience at least once in a lifetime?

_____
_____
_____

Do you have any serious regrets? What are they?

_____
_____
_____

What would you want to tell your younger self today?

_____
_____
_____
_____
_____
_____

What life experience has impacted you the most?

_____

_____

_____

Do you believe in miracles? Have you ever experienced one?

_____

_____

_____

_____

How do you find inner strength in times of struggle?

_____

_____

_____

_____

What is the one thing that always makes you feel better when you're sad?

_____

_____

_____

_____

_____

What fears have you had and how have you overcome them?

_____
_____
_____
_____
_____

Where were you during the 9/11 attacks?

_____
_____
_____

What do you think is the most important foundation in a friendship?

_____
_____
_____
_____

What do you consider to be a waste of money or time?

_____
_____
_____
_____

What is your worst habit?

_____
_____

What do you think your three best qualities are?

_____
_____
_____

What do you think your three worst qualities are?

_____
_____
_____

Which things make you feel stressed?

_____
_____
_____

What are you most grateful for?

_____
_____
_____
_____
_____

"The older I get, the smarter my father seems to get."

— Tim Russert

"A father is someone you look up to no matter how tall you grow."

– Unknown

My Wishes for You

Something I hope you experience in your lifetime

_____
_____
_____
_____

I wish you a relationship that…

_____
_____
_____
_____

I wish you a family that…

_____
_____
_____
_____

I wish you memories that…

_____
_____
_____
_____

I wish you a career that…

_____
_____
_____
_____

I wish you a life that…

_____
_____
_____
_____
_____

In 10 years, I hope you…

_____
_____
_____
_____

My biggest dreams for you…

_____
_____
_____
_____

To my dear Child,

_____

Sign your name

Share Your Favorite Joke

Notes

"When my father didn't have my hand, he had my back."

– Linda Poindexter

"The power of a dad in a child's life is unmatched."

– Justin Ricklefs

Thank You!

We hope you enjoyed this book and that it was everything you expected it to be.

Our mission is to bring families together and help you make special memories with your loved ones which they can cherish forever.

To keep bringing love and light to the world, we would love it if you could take a minute to leave a positive review on Amazon so that other people can enjoy this journal, just as you have.